ISLANDS

Rose Pipes

A ZOË BOOK

A ZOË BOOK

© 1998 Zoë Books Limited

Devised and produced by
Zoë Books Limited
15 Worthy Lane
Winchester
Hampshire SO23 7AB
England

First published in Great Britain in 1998 by
Zoë Books Limited
15 Worthy Lane
Winchester
Hampshire SO23 7AB

A record of the CIP data is available from the British Library.

ISBN 1 86173 020 9

Printed in Hong Kong by Midas Printing Ltd.
Editor: Kath Davies
Map: Sterling Associates
Design & Production: Sterling Associates

Photographic acknowledgments

The publishers wish to acknowledge, with thanks, the following photographic sources:

The Hutchison Library / Timothy Beddow 13; / Bernard Regent 21; Impact Photos / Geray Sweeney 6; / Piers Cavendish 7, 15, 16; / Clip Clap 8; / Dominic Sansoni 19; NHPA / Jean-Louis Le Moigne - cover inset tr; / Eric Soder 11; / Nigel J.Dennis 12; / David Middleton 17; / Stephen Krasemann 23; South American Pictures / Robert Francis 4; / Tony Morrison 9; Still Pictures / Don Hinrichson - cover background; / Mark Carwardine - cover inset bl; / Andy Crump 18; / Alan Watson 22; TRIP / M.Nichols 10; / H.Rogers 14; / A.Tovy 20; / D.Houghton 24; / John Gollop 25; Woodfall Wild Images / J. & E.Forder - title page; / Inigo Everson 26, 27, 28; / Tom Murphy 29.

The publishers have made every effort to trace the copyright holders, but if they have inadvertently overlooked any, they will be pleased to make the necessary arrangement at the first opportunity.

Contents

What and where are islands?

An island is land with water all around it. Islands may be large, like Greenland, or small, like Bardsey, off the coast of Wales.

This island is in Lake Titicaca, in South America.

Some islands are in rivers or lakes, and some are in seas or oceans.

Islands in seas and oceans may be mountain tops sticking up above the water. In warm seas there are islands made of **coral**.

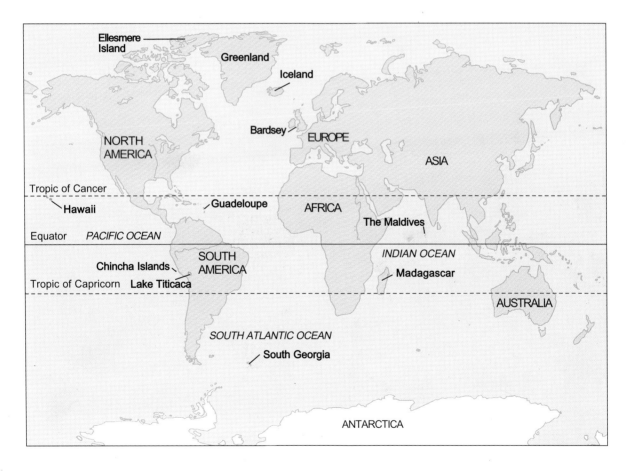

On this map, you can see the names of the islands that you will read about in this book.

Life on islands

Some islands are a long way from any other land. We call them remote islands. It may take days, or weeks, to reach remote islands by boat.

Small aircraft carry people and goods to and from some remote islands. This aircaft is on Ellesmere Island in the Arctic Ocean.

Many islanders catch and sell fish for a living. There are often fishing villages, or fishing **ports,** on island coasts.

This fishing **harbour** is on the coast of Iceland. The seas around Iceland are rich in fish such as cod and herring. Icelanders sell, or **export**, fish to other countries.

There are **holiday resorts** on many islands. The resorts bring tourists to the islands, and this helps the islanders to earn money. They find jobs in hotels and shops.

This beach is on the Caribbean island of Guadeloupe.

Before people went to live, or settled, on some islands, very few animals lived there. People brought in animals such as rats, dogs, pigs and cows.

Plant seeds are carried to islands by the wind, the sea or birds. Birds usually nest in places where they are safe from people and animals.

This is one of the Chincha Islands off the coast of Peru in South America. Brown pelicans nest here every year.

Madagascar

Madagascar is a large, **tropical** island off the east coast of Africa. It has many different **habitats**. There are forests, deserts, grasslands and high mountains.

This farmer in Madagascar uses oxen to pull his plough.

Madagascar was once joined to Africa. It separated more than 160 million years ago. The plants and animals on the island have **evolved** differently from those in Africa.

Some plants and animals here are not found anywhere else. There are special **reserves** and **National Parks** where they are protected. Tourists pay to visit these Parks.

Emperor moths, like this one, live on the island.

Baobab trees grow in Madagascar. They are well **adapted** to dry places. They store water in their trunks which swell up and look like bottles.

This baobab tree is growing in south-west Madagascar.

Baobab trees have many uses. People make rope and cloth from the bark, and paper from the wood.

Nearly 12 million people live on Madagascar. They need land for cattle, and to grow **crops** to eat and to sell. They have cleared forest habitats to make farmland. Many forest animals and plants are in danger, and may die out in 50 years' time.

This Madagascan woman is herding her ducks. You can see the rice fields behind her.

Coffee, vanilla and cloves are also grown on the island.

Iceland

Iceland is an island country near the Arctic. Deep below the ground in Iceland, the rocks are hot.

Hot rocks heat water under the ground. In some places, steam and hot water blow up out of the ground. You can see this happening in the picture.

Pipes carry hot water into people's homes, where they use it for cooking and washing. Hot water also heats greenhouses where fruit and vegetables are grown.

Hot water also flows slowly out of the ground to form pools. In this picture, people are bathing in a hot pool.

The power station behind them uses the hot water to produce electricity.

About 255,000 people live in Iceland. A main road runs all round the island. It links the villages and towns to the city of Reykjavik. The other roads are rough, so people often travel by air. There are many small airstrips on the island.

Most people live in Reykjavik, the capital city of Iceland.

Before people settled in Iceland, only one kind of **mammal** lived there. This was the Arctic fox. Now, wild reindeer and mink live there too. There are also farm animals such as cows and sheep, and dogs and other pets.

No **reptiles** live on Iceland, but there are many birds.

Some of the birds, such as this gyrfalcon, are not often seen outside Iceland.

The Maldives

The Maldives is the name of a country in the Indian Ocean. It is made up of more than 1000 small islands.

The islands are low and flat, and are all made of coral.

People live on 200 of the islands. Coconut palms and other trees and plants cover most of The Maldives. People grow fruit such as papaya and pineapples.

There is not enough space or soil to grow food crops. Most food arrives by ship.

The seas around the islands are full of fish such as bonito, tuna and swordfish. The islanders catch fish from wooden sailing boats.

Seventy of the Maldive islands are holiday resorts. The houses on these islands are built specially for visitors to stay in. People like to swim in the warm sea, and dive to see the corals and fish.

Tourists enjoy the hot, sunny weather and the beautiful beaches. They can hire boats to sail around the islands.

The world's weather is changing because of **global warming**. Some scientists think the sea level may rise by up to 38 centimetres in the next 40 years. This would drown many of the Maldive islands.

If the scientists are right, the people of The Maldives may soon have to leave their homes.

The islands in this picture may one day be below the Indian Ocean.

Hawaii

Hawaii is the largest of the Hawaiian Islands in the Pacific Ocean. There are two active **volcanoes** on Hawaii.

Hot **lava** pours out of the volcanoes when they blow up.

Hawaii Island has many different habitats. There are mountains, old lava flows, rainforests, deserts, grasslands and sandy beaches.

There are many different plants and birds on Hawaii. The brown bat was the only mammal that lived there before people arrived.

Hawaii is famous for its hibiscus flowers, and for the Hawaiian goose, or Né-Né. The goose lives high up in the hills.

Hawaii is a very popular holiday island. There are holiday resorts around the coast of Hawaii. In summer, when the weather is hot and sunny, the beaches are crowded with holiday-makers.

Tourists enjoy watching Hawaiian dances.

In winter, tourists ski in the snow-covered mountains. People also travel to Hawaii to see the volcanoes and the wildlife in the Volcanoes National Park.

Most of the land on Hawaii is used for growing crops to export to other countries. When farmers clear the land, plants and animals lose their habitats.

Farmers grow coffee, nuts, cotton and tropical fruits for export. This picture shows a field where pineapples are growing.

South Georgia

South Georgia is a small, remote island in the South Atlantic Ocean. There is snow and ice all year round here.

The only people who live on South Georgia are scientists. Here, scientists are diving from a boat.

The main plants on the island are **lichens,** mosses and tussock grass. It is too cold and snowy for trees or flowering plants to grow there.

Insects live in the grass. They are food for small birds such as the pipit. The pipit is the only songbird that lives this far south.

Sea birds nest on South Georgia. These birds are grey-headed albatrosses.

Many different kinds of seal and penguin live on South Georgia. These animals eat fish from the sea. Seals have their young on the island.

This is a male elephant seal. Its long nose looks like an elephant's trunk.

In 1904, whale hunters set up whaling stations on the island. They brought rats and reindeer with them, and the island habitat changed.

The hunters killed fur seals as well as whales in the seas round the island. These animals almost died out, or became **extinct**.

Today, hunting is not allowed and whaling stations like the one in this picture are no longer used.

Glossary

adapted: If a plant or an animal can find everything it needs to live in a place, we say it has adapted to that place. The animals can find food and shelter, and the plants have enough food in the soil and enough water. Some plants in dry areas can store water in their stems or roots.

coral: a small sea creature. Some corals have hard casings, or skeletons, which form a kind of rock, also called coral.

crops: plants that farmers grow to use or to sell.

evolved: changed and developed from an earlier form to a different one.

export: sell and take to another country.

extinct: a kind of animal which has died out.

global warming: the warming up of the weather all around the world.

habitats: the natural home of plants or animals. Examples of habitats are deserts, forests and wetlands.

harbour: a place where boats and ships can shelter.

holiday resorts: villages or towns that people visit for holidays.

lava: very hot, melted rock which flows from deep in the earth up to the surface.

lichens: grey, green or yellow plants which spread across stones and trees.

mammal: one of a group of animals whose young feed on their mother's milk.

National Parks: laws protect these lands and their wildlife from harm.

ports: towns where ships load and unload their goods.

protected: kept safe from changes that would damage the habitats.

reptiles: a group of animals which includes snakes and lizards.

reserves: areas set aside for wildlife to live in safely.

tropical: places that are hot and wet all year are called tropical. They are close to the Tropics (shown on the map on page 5).

volcanoes: hills or mountains made when lava is blown up out of the earth.

Index